DISNEY LEARNING

MY TOP 10 DISNEY

Disney · PIXAR
TOY STORY

TOP 10s
TO INFINITY AND BEYOND

MARY LINDEEN

LERNER PUBLICATIONS ◆ MINNEAPOLIS

For Benjamin, my very best pal

Lerner Publications Company
A division of Lerner Publishing Group, Inc.
241 First Avenue North
Minneapolis, MN 55401 USA

For reading levels and more information, look up this title at
www.lernerbooks.com.

Main body text set in ITC Avant Garde Gothic 13/14.
Typeface provided by International Typeface Corp.

Library of Congress Cataloging-in-Publication Data

Names: Lindeen, Mary, author.
Title: Toy story top 10s : to infinity and beyond / Mary Lindeen.
Description: Minneapolis : Lerner Publications, 2019. | Series: My top 10
    disney | Includes bibliographical references. | Audience: Age 6–10. |
    Audience: K to Grade 3.
Identifiers: LCCN 2018012805 (print) | LCCN 2018014089 (ebook) |
    ISBN 9781541543638 (eb pdf) | ISBN 9781541539099 (lb : alk. paper)
Subjects: LCSH: Toy story (Motion picture)—Juvenile literature.
Classification: LCC PN1997.T654 (ebook) | LCC PN1997.T654 L56 2019
    (print) | DDC 791.43/72—dc23

LC record available at https://lccn.loc.gov/2018012805

Manufactured in the United States of America
1-45092-35919-7/18/2018

TABLE OF CONTENTS

HOWDY, PARTNER!

WOODY AND BUZZ LIGHTYEAR ARE FRIENDS.
They have lots of laughs together! They also argue with each other sometimes. But that's okay. Friends can disagree. They can have different opinions and feel strongly about them. Buzz and Woody are full of opinions!

This book is full of opinions too. You might agree with some of these opinions. You might disagree with some of them. Would you include the same items in each list? Maybe put some of the lists in a different order? How would you make your lists different?

Everyone is allowed to have opinions, and that includes you!

SO SADDLE UP, SETTLE IN, AND START READING!

5

TOP 10 RULES FOR BEING A TOY

★ **10** You live in the world of people.

★ **9** Don't move around people.

★ **8** Don't speak around people.

**UNLESS, OF COURSE,
THEY'VE PULLED
YOUR STRING.**

6

★ **7**

Make sure people
find you where
they left you.

6

You can speak and move on your own around animals.

THEY WON'T TELL YOUR SECRET!

DID YOU KNOW?

The *Toy Story* animators loved thinking creatively when they played with their toys as kids. They experimented with their toys, changed them, and tried to think of new and different ways to play with them.

5

Be there for your kid, even though your kid might leave you one day.

4

Don't scare your kid.

YOUR JOB IS TO HELP YOUR KID FEEL SAFE.

3

Play the way your kid wants to play.

2

Make your kid happy.

THAT'S WHAT YOU'RE HERE FOR, AFTER ALL.

1

LOVE YOUR KID.

THAT'S WHAT YOUR KID IS HERE FOR, AFTER ALL.

7

TOP 10 ALIEN ADVENTURES

10 Acting in *Romeo and Juliet* with Mr. Pricklepants.

9 Being chosen by "The claaaaaaaw!"

8 Ending up in the city dump after trying to escape Sunnyside Daycare.

7 Getting kidnapped by Evil Dr. Porkchop.

"THAT'S MR. EVIL DR. PORKCHOP TO YOU!"

6

Playing with toddlers in the Caterpillar Room at Sunnyside Daycare.

5

Flying out the window of the Pizza Planet truck on the race to the airport.

HOLD ON! MR. POTATO HEAD WILL SAVE YOU!

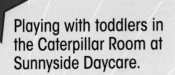

∧∧∧∧∧
DID YOU KNOW?

To make the voices for the aliens, actors inhaled helium gas before speaking their lines. Helium is used to make balloons float in the air. Inhaling helium makes a person's voice sound high and squeaky.

4

Becoming a chew toy for Sid's dog Scud.

3

Driving the getaway car for One-Eyed Bart and One-Eyed Betty.

STEP ON IT!

2

Going through the "mystic portal" at the airport.

1

USING A CRANE TO SAVE THE OTHER TOYS FROM THE FURNACE.

THEY WERE ETERNALLY GRATEFUL.

TOP 10 THINGS YOU NEED TO BE A COWBOY SHERIFF

10 A pair of blue jeans and a plaid western shirt.

9 A desire to do the right thing.

8 A red bandana.

IT KEEPS DUST FROM THE TRAIL OFF YOUR NECK.

7 A belt with a big buckle.

THE BIGGER THE BUCKLE, THE BETTER!

6

Some good sheriff catchphrases, like "Reach for the sky!"

5

A trusty horse to ride.

GIDDYAP, BULLSEYE!

4 The right cowboy hat.

3 A cowgirl for a friend. **IT'S EVEN BETTER IF SHE YODELS.**

2

A pair of cowboy boots with spurs.

1

A STAR-SHAPED SHERIFF'S BADGE.

←

TOP 10 THINGS YOU NEED TO BE A SPACE RANGER

10 The determination to help and protect people.

9 A jet pack.

8 A spaceship.

7 Arms with karate-chop action for showing off your martial arts training. **OR CHOPPING BRANCHES OUT OF THE WAY.**

6

A flip-open voice recorder for mission entries.

∧ ∧ ∧ ∧ ∧

DID YOU KNOW?

A light-year is the measure of how far light can travel in a year. How far is that? Well, that's almost 6 trillion miles (10 trillion km). It would take a person 225 million years to walk that far!

5

A job working for Star Command.

4

A space ranger badge.

IT LETS EVERYONE IN THE GALAXY KNOW YOU'RE ONE OF THE GOOD GUYS.

3

Pop-out glider wings with landing lights.

USEFUL FOR BOTH FLYING AND FALLING.

2

A blinking wrist laser.

1

A SPACE HELMET.

TOY STORY'S TOP 10 ACTION SCENES

10
Stinky Pete traps Woody and won't let him leave.

9
The toys work together to scare Sid.

8
Buzz and Woody get trapped in Sid's room.

7
Lotso drags Woody into a dumpster, and the other toys jump in to save him.

THAT'S WHAT FRIENDS DO!

6 Buzz battles the Evil Emperor Zurg on top of the elevator.

WHAT'S UP? SOMEBODY IS GOING DOWN!

∧∧∧∧∧
DID YOU KNOW?

Pixar animators had a scare when their computer system suddenly began deleting all the work they'd done on *Toy Story 2*. Fortunately, one of the animators had copied the files and taken them home. She saved the day—and the movie!

5 Woody and Buzz try to catch up to the moving van.

THEY "DROP IN" ON ANDY JUST IN TIME!

4 It's the good guys versus the bad guys in a Wild West showdown to save a train full of orphans.

3 Buzz and the other toys rescue Woody, Jessie, and Bullseye at the airport.

2 In an epic battle, Zurg blasts Buzz in half.

OUCH!

1

WOODY, BUZZ, AND THEIR FRIENDS GET CLOSER AND CLOSER TO THE FLAMES OF THE FURNACE.

LUCKILY, THE ALIENS SAVED THEM WITH A HELPING HAND, ER, CLAW.

TOP 10 TOY STORY QUOTES

10 "Ride like the wind, Bullseye!"
YEE-HAW, WOODY!

9 "This is no time to panic." —Buzz
"This is the *perfect* time to panic!" —Woody

8 "You are a sad, strange little man, and you have my pity." —Buzz

7 "The important thing is that we stick together." —Buzz

6

When Buzz starts speaking
Spanish to Jessie:
"Did you fix Buzz?" —Jessie
"Eh, sort of." —Hamm

5

"This isn't flying. This
is falling with style!"

**EITHER WAY, IT'S A
GOOD THING BUZZ
HAS THOSE WINGS!**

↳»

4

"But the thing that makes
Woody special is he'll never
give up on you . . . ever."

**ANDY KNOWS HE HAS
A FRIEND IN WOODY.**

3

"You. Are. A. TOY!" —Woody

2

"Over in that house is a kid who
thinks you are the greatest. And
it's not because you're a Space
Ranger. It's because you're a toy.
You are his toy." —Woody

1

"TO INFINITY
AND BEYOND!"

**WE ALL KNOW THIS
ONE FROM BUZZ!**

QUIZ BREAK!

Find out how much you know about the adventures of Woody, Buzz, and their friends. To the first question and beyond!

1

WOODY SAYS ALL OF THESE PHRASES WHEN YOU PULL HIS STRING, EXCEPT

A "There's a snake in my boot!"
B "Reach for the sky!"
C "You're my favorite deputy!"
D "Howdy, little lady!"

2

WHEN BUZZ FALLS OUT OF THE WINDOW, ANDY'S TOYS TRY TO SAVE HIM WITH

A A yo-yo
B A barrel of monkeys
C A jump rope
D Soldiers

3

BUZZ HAS ALL OF THE FOLLOWING FEATURES EXCEPT

A Chopping action
B A glow-in-the-dark suit
C Flying abilities
D Laser beam light

4

WHEN BUZZ MEETS THE ALIENS AT PIZZA PLANET, WHO OR WHAT DO THEY CLAIM IS THEIR MASTER?

A Buzz
B Zurg
C The claw
D Pizza

5

AL'S TOY BARN COMMERCIALS FEATURE

A Al dressed as a chicken
B Giant stuffed animals
C Al doing the chicken dance
D Al sitting on a rocking horse

6

WHAT IS THE NAME OF JESSIE'S PREVIOUS KID?

A Molly
B Amanda
C Amy
D Emily

7

WHO DID WOODY SAVE FROM THE YARD SALE?

A Wheezy
B Bo's sheep
C Hamm
D Squeaky shark

8

BONNIE FIRST FINDS WOODY

A When she trips over him
B Hanging from a tree
C In a box
D In the Caterpillar Room

9

WHOSE IDEA WAS IT TO CLIMB INSIDE THE SUNNYSIDE DONATION BOX?

A Buzz
B Jessie
C Mr. Potato Head
D Woody

10

WHO RESCUED ANDY'S TOYS AT THE TRI-COUNTY LANDFILL?

A The aliens
B Lotso
C Zurg
D A landfill worker

TOP 10 TIMES TOY STORY MADE US CRY

10 When Chuckles tells the story of how he, Big Baby, and Lotso ended up at Sunnyside Daycare.

9 Buster changes and grows older just as Andy does. When Andy leaves for college, he hopes Buster will still be around the next time he comes home.

8 Woody chooses to stay at Al's and refuses to go back to Andy with the other toys.

OH, WOODY, PLEASE GO WITH YOUR OLD FRIENDS.

7 Then Woody realizes he'll miss Andy if he doesn't go home.

OH, WOODY, DON'T LEAVE YOUR NEW FRIENDS AT AL'S!

6

Buzz realizes that he's a toy.

HE HAS A BROKEN ARM . . . AND A BROKEN HEART.

5

Woody decides to leave Sunnyside and says goodbye to everyone, including Bullseye.

4

Jessie tells Woody about Emily outgrowing her.

DOES ANYONE HAVE A TISSUE?

3

When all the toys quietly hold hands (and paws and hooves and claws) as they get closer to the flames of the furnace.

2

When Andy gives his toys to Bonnie.

1

∧∧∧∧∧

DID YOU KNOW?

Music can help people connect to their emotions. Music often tells a movie audience whether a scene is sad, exciting, funny, or scary. The songs from the Toy Story movies also help the audience know what the characters think and feel.

THE TOYS WATCH ANDY DRIVE AWAY AS HE HEADS OFF TO COLLEGE. "SO LONG, PARTNER . . ."

←

TOY STORY'S TOP 10 FUNNY MOMENTS

10 Woody knocks Buzz's space helmet off, and Buzz thinks he can't breathe.

9 Jessie skateboards down a ramp, yodels, launches herself onto the doorknob, and opens the door so Buster can go outside "for a little private time."

BUZZ IS SO IMPRESSED THAT HIS WINGS POP UP!

8 When Woody and Buzz meet each other for the first time.

"HELLOOO—AHH!"

7 The aliens' excitement about being chosen by the claw.

OOOOOH!

6

Tour Guide Barbie drives the toys through Al's Toy Barn.

BUCKLE UP!

5

Woody asks Buzz to give him a hand in Sid's room, and Buzz throws him a whole arm.

GOOD ONE, BUZZ.

4

The toys work together to drive the Planet Pizza truck to the airport.

3

The toys use orange traffic cones to "safely" cross the street.

2

Spanish-mode Buzz dancing with Jessie. *¡Olé!*

1

BUZZ, WEARING A PINK APRON AND A FLOWERED HAT, DROWNS HIS SORROWS AT A TEA PARTY.

"YOU SEE THE HAT? I AM MRS. NESBITT!" 23

TOP 10 THINGS ANDY LEARNS FROM HIS TOYS

10 **HOW TO DECORATE A ROOM.**

First, a cowboy bedspread and then a space ranger bedspread.

9 **HOW TO DEVELOP HIS ARTISTIC SKILLS.**

Buzz and Woody inspire a lot of Andy's drawings.

→»

8 **HOW TO USE HIS IMAGINATION.**

That's where Evil Dr. Porkchop and One-Eyed Betty come from!

7 **HOW TO HAVE HOPE.**

Woody and Buzz were lost, but they found their way back to him!

6

HOW TO TRUST.

Toys are friendly, not scary.

5

HOW TO BE CARING.

Andy takes good care of his toys. He fixed Woody's torn arm.

^ ^ ^ ^ ^

DID YOU KNOW?

Andy isn't the only kid who grows up in the Toy Story movies. Sid grows up to be the garbage collector in *Toy Story 3*. Did you catch that?

4

HOW TO SHARE.

Bonnie will have so much fun with Andy's toys!

3

HOW TO BE LOYAL.

As Andy says, Woody will never give up on you.

2

HOW TO BE DEPENDABLE.

The toys are always there for Andy when he needs them.

1

HOW TO BE GRATEFUL.

"THANKS, GUYS."

TOP 10 TOY STORY CONNECTIONS TO OTHER MOVIES

10

THE WIZARD OF OZ

Just like Dorothy, Woody says, "There's no place like home," when he's trying to get out of Sid's room.

9

STAR WARS

The loud breathing sound Buzz makes when wearing his space helmet is similar to Darth Vader's famous breathing sound.

8

A BUG'S LIFE

Heimlich the caterpillar is on one of the branches being chopped by Buzz.

7

STAR WARS: EPISODE V— THE EMPIRE STRIKES BACK

Zurg tells Buzz, "I am your father," which is the same thing Darth Vader says to Luke Skywalker.

6

CARS

A toy car that looks like Lightning McQueen is at Sunnyside Daycare.

5

FINDING NEMO

Bonnie has a bandage with Dory on it, and Dory is in some of the paintings at the day care.

4

THE INCREDIBLES

In *Toy Story 3*, the model jet in Andy's room looks just like the one that Elastigirl pilots to save Mr. Incredible from Syndrome's island.

THE LION KING

2

"Hakuna Matata" is playing on the car radio as Andy, his sister, and his mom drive to their new house.

^^^^^
DID YOU KNOW?

The Pizza Planet truck from *Toy Story* shows up in all the Toy Story movies. It appears in lots of other movies too, including *Cars*, *Finding Nemo*, *Inside Out*, and *Coco*. Hidden connections in a movie are called Easter Eggs because you have to hunt for them!

3

A BUG'S LIFE

Mrs. Potato Head is shown reading *A Bug's Life* storybook.

1 ⟪ ⟵

CARS

ON THE WAY TO PIZZA PLANET, ANDY'S MOM PULLS INTO A DINOCO GAS STATION.

TOP 10 FRIENDSHIP FACTS FROM BUZZ AND WOODY

10 Friends don't always like each other when they first meet.

"LISTEN, LIGHTSNACK, YOU STAY AWAY FROM ANDY. HE'S MINE, AND NO ONE IS TAKING HIM AWAY FROM ME." —WOODY

9 You can have more than one good friend.

ANDY'S NAME IS ON WOODY'S BOOT AND BUZZ'S BOOT.

8 Friends give each other a helping hand.

AND SOMETIMES THAT HAND IS ATTACHED TO AN ARM.

7 Friends don't give up on each other.

"THE IMPORTANT THING IS THAT WE STICK TOGETHER." —BUZZ

6

Friends tell each other the truth.

5

Friends protect each other.

^^^^^
DID YOU KNOW?

A toy can become a kid's best friend. Toy designers know how to make toys that kids will love. It takes creativity, artistic talent, design skills, and hard work to become an expert toy maker. But when you go to work, you get to spend your days playing with toys and thinking like a kid!

4

Friends can argue and still be friends.

3

Friends can be different from each other.

FOR EXAMPLE, ONE CAN BE A COWBOY AND ONE CAN BE A SPACE RANGER.

2

Friends have fun together.

1

THE BEST WAY TO HAVE A GOOD FRIEND IS TO BE A GOOD FRIEND.

YOU'VE GOT A FRIEND IN ME!

MAKE YOUR OWN TOY STORY TOP 10!

NOW IT'S YOUR TURN TO MAKE A TOP 10 LIST. Make a copy of the blank list on the next page. Then write your own Toy Story Top 10 list. You can change one of the lists in this book. Or you can make a new list, such as

• JESSIE'S TOP 10 QUOTES

• THE TOP 10 QUESTIONS I'D LIKE TO ASK THE PEOPLE WHO MADE TOY STORY

The choices are endless—they stretch to infinity and beyond!

MY

TOP 10:

10. _____

9. _____

8. _____

7. _____

6. _____

5. _____

4. _____

3. _____

2. _____

1. _____

TO LEARN MORE

Books

Boothroyd, Jennifer. *How to Be a Beloved Toy: Teamwork with Woody*. Minneapolis: Lerner Publications, 2019. Being a toy sheriff can be a tough job! Read this book to learn about everything that goes into a day's work for Woody.

Junior Encyclopedia of Animated Characters. New York: Disney, 2014. From Buzz to Woody to all your other favorite Toy Story toys, this book gives you more fun facts, trivia, and quotes from Disney's animated characters.

Websites

Disney Pixar Toy Story
http://toystory.disney.com
From games to videos to picture galleries, this website will welcome you to the Toy Story world.

Overview of Pixar in a Box
https://www.khanacademy.org/partner-content/pixar/start/introduction/v/pipeline-video
Go inside the Pixar studios with this video showing how animators use technology and innovation to create movie magic.